WINNERS WIN
LOSERS MAKE EXCUSES

BY **JON ROBERT QUINN**

WINNERS WIN. LOSERS MAKE EXCUSES.

Page 3 | Introduction

Page 7 | Why Winners Win

Page 13 | Failure Isn't an Option

Page 23 | Hold Yourself Accountable

Page 27 | Becoming Valuable

Page 33 | Losers Make Excuses

Page 38 | Finding Positive Energy

Page 44 | Your Circle

Page 49 | Believing Your Bullshit

Page 57 | A New Start

Page 66 | Quit Making Excuses

WINNERS WIN. LOSERS MAKE EXCUSES.

Introduction

This book needed to be written because every single day a business professional or entrepreneur comes to me with a problem, I give them the answer or point them in right direction and a lot of times, they never do anything with it. I know this is not just me who deals with this. This is a problem that plagues the workforce and if I can help even one person, this book was worth it.

You cannot be successful if every opportunity presented to you slips through your fingers. You have to do the work. You cannot think and grow rich. You have to DO to grow rich. You have to get off your ass and make something of yourself. Why do winners

WINNERS WIN. LOSERS MAKE EXCUSES.

win? And, why do losers always have an excuse for losing? I guess it's all a matter of perspective and what you want to accomplish in life. The sad thing is, there isn't a section for books on mediocrity in the bookstore or library. You're reading this book because you want to be successful. Chances are, you're already successful and don't even know it yet and I say that because you're feeding your brain with knowledge which is the first step of success.

Many entrepreneurs have this idea of what they want, but don't know how to get there and end up spending their lives chasing something that is unrealistic. They look at Instagram and see all these people with Bentleys and Mansions and Louis Vuitton bags. This is a very unrealistic way of looking at life considering those are all either actors or trust fund babies.

WINNERS WIN. LOSERS MAKE EXCUSES.

I consider myself successful, but in the eyes of people chasing shiny objects, I probably look like a failure to them. But I will say that I make my living writing books, music and producing movies and I don't have record companies, publishers or movie studios barking orders at me. I just do my thing and live comfortably in Northern California. I have the toys I want and my wife and dog and great group of friends and colleagues. It's a great life. It took a shit ton of work to get here, but I'm here. The point is, I did it. I did the work. And, I am doing what I want to do with my life, not what society says I need to be doing.

This book is going to be an interesting read for sure. There will be parts that are motivational and parts that will make you think, hopefully helping you get focused. My gift of writing and educating is not here to hurt people's feelings or put people down. Some things I will say in this book will be shocking.

WINNERS WIN. LOSERS MAKE EXCUSES.

They will probably hurt some feelings and at times, I may sound like an asshole. But, that is not my intention.

I want to inspire and motivate and sometimes things needs to be said in a way that strikes a nerve. You're in control of your life. I simply want to help you accomplish the things you want in life. Sadly, most people fail simply because they make excuses for themselves. It's time to put those bad habits behind you and create accomplishments you've only dreamt of.

WINNERS WIN. LOSERS MAKE EXCUSES.

Why Winners Win

In thinking about why winners win, only one real thing comes to mind, determination. The other night I watched a video of Ed Sheeran on YouTube talking about how people have always said he had natural-born talent. His response was, "no I didn't" and proceeded to show a video from years prior. He was terrible. It was comical. He went on to say that talent is only a small piece of it. Practice makes perfect but the wrong practice makes you really good at being not good.

When I was getting my start in music, I practiced guitar nine hours a day for years to become as good as I was. I'm not nearly as good today as I was in my twenties, but I also don't really practice much anymore. I still cut an album every couple of years and will spend a few months getting my hands reconditioned so I can get back to recording, but I assure you, it doesn't happen naturally.

Looking back at Michael Jordan, his coaches had coaches. He was the hardest working player on the court and look at where that led him. Had he just half assed his efforts, LeBron would be the greatest of all time. See what I did there? Jordan was a force. He was a phenomenon, BUT he had to do the work. Bo Jackson was another one. In my opinion, he was the most versatile athlete of his time. Most of us know that he played both Baseball and Football and was quite good at both, but what a lot of people don't know is that he was a great businessman too. Let's just say, 'Bo Knows Best'. Bo was approaching merchandise companies and negotiating endorsements way before anybody else was doing it and he was maintaining control of his name and intellectual properties when everybody else was signing their names away.

Another legendary athlete is Jerry Rice. At practice, he would be thrown the ball and would run all the way to the end zone with the ball. When asked why he doesn't just return the ball, he said catching balls doesn't lead to touchdowns, running the ball leads to touchdowns. This simple concept made him one of the best the game had ever seen. He had a winner's mentality and made sure he was going to win. It's one thing to become a professional. It's another to become great.

When you're thinking about your business, you have to do what is necessary to win. If you want to get your business off the ground and you're spending more time watching television than building your

WINNERS WIN. LOSERS MAKE EXCUSES.

business, then maybe it's time to throw your television away. My wife and I did this a number of years ago and what a difference it made in our home. No television does not mean that we work all the time. We play cards or read or take drives and even throw on an episode of our favorite show while we eat dinner, but our time is constructive. The information we put into our brains is of quality. We also got rid of social media. Personally, I think social media is what is killing society. It makes people stupid.

Social media forces us to NOT think and focuses our energy on things that don't provide any value into our times. And the argument that you need it for your business is just an excuse. I deleted TikTok first and found myself spending less time looking at nonsense and clearing my brain of garbage. Then came Twitter when I saw them silencing people. Then came Instagram when I saw them forcing me to look at things I didn't have an interest in. And finally came Facebook when I saw people arguing with each other on Christmas. I thought for sure I would go through withdrawals losing Facebook. At first, I wasn't sure how long it would last. It's been months now and I have not looked back. What a difference it made in my life.

When I got off of social media, of course my friends reached out asking if I was ok and were questioning whether I was losing my mind. After a couple months, they saw my entire life changing and now they are trying it. The other day, one of my closest friends told me he did the same thing and feels like a million bricks off his shoulders. He's feeding his mind with what he wants rather than what the system THINKS he wants.

If you're meeting with quality people throughout the week and you provide exceptional service, you will find plenty of great referrals helping your business thrive.

Remember, you are who you surround yourself with. If you surround yourself around drama, you will find yourself with more problems than you can shake a stick at. If you surround yourself with people who want to win and are doing what is necessary to win, you will find yourself winning. However, if you're chasing the illusion of a shiny object, you will never win in your mind because you will always be chasing. We will get deeper into this later.

Failure Isn't an Option

Time and time again I tell entrepreneurs to be relentless. They must stand up when everybody else sits down. They must do what everybody else is afraid to do. If your competition is marketing their businesses on social media, then you must do billboards or radio. If everybody is buying a Tesla, then buy a Mercedes. If everybody else is wearing shorts, then wear jeans. I recently read an article in Gentleman's Journal about Gianni Agnelli. When he would go to the gym, he would wear jeans. I'm sure in the moment, they looked at him like he was a mad man, but it's what was comfortable to him. All these years later, he's the one these magazines write articles about. Steve McQueen is another one.

The problem with conforming with the norm is that you blend into the mix leaving little to be desired. You can have a great product and a great delivery, but if you cannot communicate your message effectively, people won't even realize you're standing there right in front of them. Failure is not an option. I want to tell you a little story about something that happened recently to me that really opened my eyes showing me I was in the right place and also, how much I have grown and how far I have come.

Many many years ago, I was going bankrupt. My retail stores had closed and I about ready to forfeit my apartment. I pretty much had sold everything to cover bills and it just wasn't enough. The problem wasn't that I was lazy or wasn't doing the right things,

I'm positive there were plenty of mistakes made along the way. I can think of about a dozen off the top of my head. But, that's how we learn. That's how we overcome. The problem was, I wasn't 'there' yet. I wasn't in the right place for that moment in my life. Education is very expensive. Think of the trials of entrepreneurship like college for business visionaries. Every semester has a variety of lessons and those lessons cost money and if you're not willing to invest the time and money to learn what you need to to survive, you're not going to graduate.

Once I closed my retail stores in 2012, everything pretty much stopped. I had online orders coming in, but it wasn't enough. I had sold one of my cars to open the store, so that was now gone. I sold my guitars. I sold my furniture. The next thing to let go was accruing business expenses. My domain JonRobertQuinn.com was next as I was no longer

WINNERS WIN. LOSERS MAKE EXCUSES.

using it for the business. Come 2013, I was living out of my car from my second big business failure. My first happened at age twenty and here I was thirty years old, broke and homeless...again. I spoke to my mother and told her I think it's time to hang up my hat and retire the Jon Robert Quinn brand. It just wasn't working. I was back to square one and it had already been around fourteen years at this time since launching my first music album. I was a failure in the world's eyes.

By thirty, I was living in my car but had released five or six music albums, had a website design business that was in the toilet, had worked with Jay Leno and the Ferrari parts business was dead because during the Great Recession, who was buying Ferrari parts? The argument is, well the Ferrari dealer was selling parts. Of course they were. They're the Ferrari dealer. I was seeing guys with entire

WINNERS WIN. LOSERS MAKE EXCUSES.

Ferrari collections being repossessed. It was a crazy time. It just wasn't my time. I was still learning at the school of hard knocks.

Mid 2013, I got a job in sales and actually did quite well. I have talked about my employment accomplishments in other books, so I won't go into it too much here. However, it wasn't maybe six months when I was getting the itch again to start another business and re-establish the Jon Robert Quinn brand. The issue though was that some chinese company had purchased and registered the JonRobertQuinn.com domain and wanted to sell it back to me at a premium for over $3000. I chose JonRobertQuinn.org and went back to work building my brand with new books and music and even opened another motorcycle shop.

WINNERS WIN. LOSERS MAKE EXCUSES.

The years would pass and radio shows came into the mix. Jon Robert Quinn products started popping up on eBay for three to four times retail pricing. My old CDs from a decade earlier also started popping up on collector sites. It was all finally starting to happen. Mid 2015 was a turning point for me. The Good Life Show with Jon Robert Quinn premiered on 105.5 FM in Sacramento, also later airing in Seattle, Denver and Miami. In 2016, I was voted number one FM Radio in Sacramento. One night I was driving home, I turned on the radio and on came the Jon Robert Quinn song, City Lights. I look up at the downtown buildings and think of the day I wrote that song and the meaning and that's when I knew I made it. I was now the big time. I presented for the Sacramento Kings halftime show. I was being asked to do cameos in movies. It was an awesome time.

WINNERS WIN. LOSERS MAKE EXCUSES.

Fast-forward another eight years and it's where I sit today. I left radio to build podcasts and television. I started filmmaking about three years ago and focusing on my IMDB channel rather than my YouTube channel. I'm now producing and directing movies. I have worked with many great actors in Hollywood and produced some great films. I have held off on writing music in the past year, but still have recordings being released that were in queue. I write a lot of books. Books and movies is really where my passion is these days. And that motorcycle shop I reopened a number of years ago to prove to myself, I wasn't a failure, I built it into a great little web-series called Knuckleheads on IMDB. Had I given up, I wouldn't be where I am at today.

So, back to my JonRobertQuinn.com story. The other night, I was going through Jon Robert Quinn search results on Google and sending 'friendly' emails

WINNERS WIN. LOSERS MAKE EXCUSES.

to the companies posting content on Jon Robert Quinn that don't have authority to do so, and I came across an old forum post from around 2005. That being a lifetime ago, I had to stop and read and think about where I was in that moment. At the end of the forum post, it mentioned JonRobertQuinn.com, so I clicked on it and NOTHING. I clicked again and NOTHING. Immediately, I went to SquareSpace and made the purchase. Those people that owned it, I guess gave up and never renewed it and I got my original domain back. This is where I realized the importance of never giving up.

The next morning I called Matt. You may know him from our show Talking Sh*t with Matt & Quinn and he's also associate producer for the High Rise movie franchise we've been building. He made the comment that he was surprised that I didn't own .com as I had been using .org as long as we've known each other.

WINNERS WIN. LOSERS MAKE EXCUSES.

In the moment, I couldn't remember why I was using .org and had to think about it. I told him that this was the point in my life where I had given up all hope and let it everything go. I was done. I was retiring the Jon Robert Quinn brand and had nothing left in me to give the world. This was the moment I realized my lesson and knew I had to share this story with the world.

Failure is not an option, yet it's ok to fail as long as you don't give up. Failing and failing again is part of the journey, but failing and walking away makes you a failure. Nobody wants to be a failure. As entrepreneurs, we hear story after story of overnight success that take twenty years to accomplish. The story of Colonial Sanders and being turned down over and over until he finally got a yes. These stories are everywhere. How many visionaries never got their moment because they just gave up on themselves. I

WINNERS WIN. LOSERS MAKE EXCUSES.

was one of them. I gave up. I was done. Something in me told me to get back up and try again and here I am today, you're reading my book and thank you for that.

Hold Yourself Accountable

Half of your problems start by not holding yourself accountable. I do it too. I think it's just a part of entrepreneurship. There are days I just don't want to work. It seems like a better idea to hop into the car and drive to the beach for the day. But realistically, we cannot do that every day. I mean, we can, but we shouldn't. You give yourself work to do and then just don't want to get it done. Yet, when it's done, you feel great because you've accomplished something.

You also don't want to give yourself unrealistic expectations like saying you'll only work a hundred hours this week. That isn't responsible. You're killing yourself with that nonsense. You need a proper balance between work life and home life. Read my book *4-Hour Work Day* for great tips on how to get more enjoyment out of life, yet still staying focused on your work. The take away from the book is that we as human ONLY have about four good hours of work in us each day. The rest of the time, we're not focussed or finding ways to pass the time and there are a lot of studies on this.

I work closely with a lot of professionals and there are a lot of times me and the client will set a schedule on what needs done and when. First, they have trouble paying the invoice. Next, they have trouble making the appointments. And before long, they aren't answering phone calls or texts from me. They just lost interest. And the sad part isn't that they lost interest in something that would be a hobby, this is their business. Not only that, they spent the money and threw it away. I think to myself, how many other times has this happened? Is this a pattern for them? It's no wonder why entrepreneurs fail. If they are just giving up and not following through on the easy stuff, how will they make it through the hard stuff?

Business isn't easy and sometimes it's not fun. You're not always going to win. Yet, when you do, everything feels like a win. As does failing. You can win regularly and fail once, then give up and everything becomes a failure. So, where do you start?

When you commit, follow through. Do what you say you're going to do. There was a scene in the movie Armageddon that resonated with me all those years ago. At the end of the film, Harry Stamper had to detonate the nuke on the astroid and something was said when Colonial Sharp wasn't sure if he'd get it done. The quote was something to the effect of, "Harry doesn't know how to miss his mark."

WINNERS WIN. LOSERS MAKE EXCUSES.

The entire movie fell on that moment of his follow through and I have always told myself to follow that level of commitment on any engagement I have. In my book *Accountability: Show Up and Win* I talk about showing up to appointments an hour early just in case life happens. We never know when were going to get a flat tire or have to use the restroom or get pulled over, so account for those things and arrive early. Work from the car if you have to until your scheduled meeting time. You will be relaxed and not rushed and you can always make calls or answer emails from the car. The irony is that in this moment of me writing this book, I am early for our networking event Network Nites at House of Oliver in Granite Bay, California. There is nothing more disrespectful that showing up late to an appointment.

WINNERS WIN. LOSERS MAKE EXCUSES.

Becoming Valuable

We as entrepreneurs, most times, don't know our worth. I have written about this subject in many books over the years. Value = Value. You will become more valuable to others as you invest more into yourself. If you're always cutting corners and putting out a shitty product, you'll find yourself with less and less clients and wondering how you'll pay your bills. Eventually, you will be out of business.

The problem is that most people do not realise that they are the problem. They bounce from one business idea to the next, never investing in themself and when something doesn't work, they try something else. There are two problems with this.

Problem one is that they haven't given the idea enough time or energy to make it successful. They are looking for fast results. You see this a lot in MLM (Multi-Level Marketing) professionals and as well in real estate professionals, ie: realtors and lenders.

Problem two is that most entrepreneurs start thinking about their next big idea when what they are doing isn't working. They start something new and try that for a little bit and it doesn't work like they expect, and they start something else. This pattern follows them throughout their entire entrepreneurial career until they fail and they fail because they never gave enough of themselves to any of their ideas.

When you're doing too many things, you're not able to give enough of yourself for it to work. You're spreading yourself too thin. Your ego is getting in the way and you want to feel like a super hero, but instead you're making pennies with one idea and dimes with another. Eventually, you're looking for next idea because you have bills to pay and become desperate. I see this all too often.

Instead of trying EVERYTHING, focus on your passion. What do you love to do that you would do for free? Do that! As you're able to build a name for yourself in that industry, you'll find yourself getting offers to help others. These offers will start small and become larger and larger until you're able to pick and choose who you want to work with and how often you want to work.

I started writing music when I was in my early twenties and didn't make much money at all. Everybody used to tell me to get a job and earn a real living, but I enjoyed producing music. The funny thing now is that I make the same money on my music I did twenty years ago, but I don't have to do all that work anymore. I just collect royalty checks for the songs I wrote because that music gets streamed on Apple Music, Spotify, TikTok, YouTube, TV and Movies and a myriad of other places. Now, when people ask me how I make a living and I tell them from intellectual properties, they stare at me in confusion. The idea of not trading time for money is greek to most people. Next, they seem to always ask about my retirement and what I will do in my later years.

What's really fucked up about this is, first off, who's business is it of who's what your retirement plan is and second, 95% of Americans who are saving for retirement will have nothing for retirement simply because of inflation. Let's say they save a million dollars. In thirty years, that will get them through maybe two or three years.

WINNERS WIN. LOSERS MAKE EXCUSES.

The other part of this is that I still write music, as well as books and movies and radio shows and podcasts. I own a website design business and we help companies with digital media. All of this creates passive income, yet I do what I WANT for a living rather than what society says I need to do and all these naysayers out there with their $1000 car payments and boat payments and high credit card debt and multiple mortgages pissing away every cent they make while they trade time for money are giving you financial advice. Do what YOU want to do. If you want to sell popcorn, then sell popcorn. Just remember to give the business what it needs and follow your passion through and if you don't invest in yourself, you'll never become more valuable to the client or customer.

Another thing to think about with creating multiple business strategies is the time/cost analysis.

WINNERS WIN. LOSERS MAKE EXCUSES.

This is very very important. If one business takes two hours a day and makes twenty percent of your monthly income, then you need to focus on that. The problem is that most people are spending all of their time on ideas that make no money and not enough time on ideas that make good money. Then, out of desperation, they add something else into the mix hurting the one business that is actually producing income.

If you have a business and home life such has wife and kids, you have to remember that 50% of your time will be devoted to your family and the other 50% to your business. When you add another business, you're now cutting 50% down to 33% and adding another cuts that down to 25%. Your family gets less and less time and here is a prime example of why divorce rates are so high. You have to create a positive work and life balance.

WINNERS WIN. LOSERS MAKE EXCUSES.

Losers Make Excuses

Want to fail? Then keep making excuses for yourself. When I was a kid, my uncle would ask me why I didn't get the dishes done or take out the trash and I always had a clever excuse and I learned at a very young age that excuses are bullshit. I give a task to real estate client and some always find an excuse as to why it didn't get done. Or, we will have an appointment to shoot video or do photos and they will have a 'reason' they can't make the appointment. I always ask myself, if I was the President, would these people still miss the appointment? Probably not! So, am I not valuable to them? Hell, they paid the invoice, so what difference does it make. I still got paid.

WINNERS WIN. LOSERS MAKE EXCUSES.

The sad thing is, people are creatures of habit. This is normal behaviour to them. It's no wonder why so many professionals fail. They miss deadlines and miss appointments and are late on their bills and when they come across somebody that has their shit together, they either envy that person or despise that person. I guess it all comes down to how they look at success. It's like the kid in high school that always has their homework turned in on time being the teacher's pet. No, they just have their shit together.

I've said this before and I will say it again, I think social media and television are the biggest problem we have in society today. Not drugs or guns, but television and social media. I feel this way because we as a society stare at the idiot box for hours and hours living our lives through the shiny colours on the screen. And here I am making mobster movies. I am part of the problem, I guess. I think the

WINNERS WIN. LOSERS MAKE EXCUSES.

bigger problem is what people are focussing their energy on. Are they watching ten minutes of television after dinner to wind down or wasting their evening away binge watching whatever is being fed to them. Everything in moderation, right?

They are watching the news and watching serial killer programs and shows on making drugs and programs with violence and filling their brains with more and more garbage. And then before bed, they scroll social media and see that the Jones' down the street just bought a new boat and now they want one. And then they take interest in the drama between this person and that person and who's getting divorced. We as a society are getting dumber and dumber. We waste our time watching the idiot box. We no longer think for ourselves. We're being programmed by society to believe and think a certain way and that culturally, is a very scary thing.

WINNERS WIN. LOSERS MAKE EXCUSES.

The complacency as a society saying that it's ok to be late to work and the job will get done if we pass the torch onto somebody else rather than holding ourselves accountable and getting the job done is why so many people are continuing to struggle. We don't have time to write books or take classes or schedule meetings with the right people that will help our careers but we have plenty of time for the idiot box. And when we miss that deadline, we tell ourselves that "it just wasn't meant to be." It's like we have given up on ourselves before we even had the opportunity.

It's crazy to look at the lives of billionaires and their commitment to their work and ego and nothing else. Working fifteen hour days is extremely unhealthy in every aspect of your life. And all for what? Money? Seriously? But they are changing the world, right? If that's the life you want, then great. But, I can assure you, you're not reading this book if you're in the shoes of a billionaire. Or, maybe you are. However, if you want to be successful, whatever that looks like for you, then quit making excuses for yourself and do what is necessary both at work and at home.

WINNERS WIN. LOSERS MAKE EXCUSES.

Finding Positive Energy

We as entrepreneurs and professionals are constantly surrounding ourselves with people. Some of these people are the right people. These are the ones that inspire us and build us up and even challenge us. And then there are the ones that tear us down. They doubt us and question us and provide us with no real value. There is nothing more frustrating when you're making progress and the people in your circle are tearing down your every move. It's extremely detrimental. And when somebody says, "You can't to that", just remember that what they are really saying is that THEY can't do that.

We are who we surround ourselves with. If we surround ourselves around a bunch of people that are always depressed and down in the dumps, chances are they will bring us down with them. People that always have drama and bad things happening to them will drag you into their problems, again adding detriment to your life. THIS is why you're running into so many people that are making excuses for themselves. They are stuck in old habits and bleeding those habits onto you.

I was at a weird place in my life when I met my buddy Matt. We had met years and years prior but it wasn't until I was shooting video for his restaurants that I realised what I was doing to myself. I was always go go go. I was always worried about money and chasing the illusion of happiness. I didn't really know what happiness was.

WINNERS WIN. LOSERS MAKE EXCUSES.

One day I got a call and it went something like this. Ring ring…

"Hello, this is Quinn."

"Hey, it's Matt."

"What's up dude, how can I help?"

"Just saying hey. What's up?"

"I'm good bro. Busy, what's up. How can I help?"

"Nothing, just seeing how you're doing. Wanna get lunch?"

"Uh, ok. Sure. But how can I help?"

"I just want to get lunch."

I was so focused on work I wasn't seeing a good person just wanting to get to know me. There was something he was looking for, either professionally or personally and he was going after it.

WINNERS WIN. LOSERS MAKE EXCUSES.

I was so in my zone and focus, I didn't see it. We went to lunch and talked and enjoyed the conversation. We went to get lunch again a few days later and months, then years later, we're doing business together. I have taught him a lot about business and people and growth and he has taught me a lot of living and happiness. I had never met somebody that was actually happy and content. This was very new to me.

One day he sits me down and tells me I need to make some changes or I'm going to end up having a heart attack. He was right. My health was already starting to shift and I knew the stress was doing it. He coached me and made me into the relaxed, forward thinking and prosperous businessman I am today. And I got him into film and helped him build his media company.

WINNERS WIN. LOSERS MAKE EXCUSES.

We need positive people around us. We need people that will build us up and force us to think and be better. When my buddy Gary and I get together, we talk for hours and hours. We talk life and business and philosophy and politics. We always leave the sit down with something of meaning. We don't always agree with each other, but there's something special there. I mentor him and he mentors me. The funny thing is, his net worth is a hundred times what mine is and we still find value in the conversation we have together and this relationship is somewhere around sixteen to eighteen years and counting. We need more people like this around us.

So, what do we do with the people that tear us down? Do we throw them away? Yes and no. If they aren't providing any value to your life, then spend less time with them. Keep it to holidays and birthdays. If they disrespect you, maybe it's time to have a talk

WINNERS WIN. LOSERS MAKE EXCUSES.

with them and find out where the issue is. There just may be a misunderstanding. Feel it out and if there is nothing positive in the relationship, maybe it's best if both parties part ways. Maybe, as you continue to mature, there will be something for you two later down the line.

Your Circle

Setting up your circle is crucial to your success. You need different people in your circle that have different roles in your life. However, when you're setting up your circle, make sure those people aren't ass kissers. You want honest people that will build you up but also tell you when you're wrong, but do so in a respectful manner.

Think about the people you want in your life but don't overthink it. When I started writing my High Rise movies, I studied The Sopranos very deeply in how he surrounded himself with the right people. The show The Sopranos was so accurate in their storylines, that the real mob thought they were being watched by the show's writers. Business is very much like the mob. You have your accountants and your investors and your running men and your advisors. You keep things very tight lipped outside of the circle and make strategic moves that counter that of your competition.

Think of your circle like your own little mafia. It's funny, I use the term "keeping it in the family" and my circle understands what I am saying. It's important that you trust your circle and have the right people in place to handle certain tasks. Even if they aren't on payroll and are contractors, they are still in your circle. You know that when you make the call, they will be happy to hear from you and will get the job done. They will also call when they don't hear from you for a period of time and genuinely take interest in your family and interests. These are the people you need around you.

How big should your circle be? I suggest five to seven people tops in your "A" circle. You can have a "B" circle with folks that would be your second choice if your first choice isn't available and even have a "C" circle. You may over time find that your "B" contacts slowly start becoming "A" contacts. Just remember to keep your circle tight and fill it with quality.

So, we have covered your business circle, what about your personal circle? Personally, I think it's the same philosophy. I have Matt and Gary and Dante and Caleb and Frank, etc. They all have different roles in my life both at work and outside of work but regardless, I know I can count of them and I reward them by showing them how much I appreciate them. I take them to dinner or lunch, I invite them to events I am planning. We will go to baseball games. I give them kickbacks for freebees. Or, even just spend more time talking and building a stronger bond.

WINNERS WIN. LOSERS MAKE EXCUSES.

When putting your circle together, write down everybody in your life and what you love and don't love about them. Feel free to sit down with them and discuss this journey you're on and see how they want to complement your journey. Do they want to be in your "A" circle? Chances are, they feel the same about you and want you in their circle.

It was funny, I called Gary one day and said I needed to sit down with him and speak with him. We had known each other for over a decade prior and I talked to him about my circle and he expressed his concerns with some of the people he considered in his circle and we found that from two different walks of life, we both needed each other more than we realised. We now make it a point to spend at least an afternoon a month together just talking and learning from each other. No matter where somebody is at in their life, young or old, there is something to learn

WINNERS WIN. LOSERS MAKE EXCUSES.

from them. You would be surprised what you learn even talking to your ten year old nephew. You both can learn so much from each other.

Believing Your Bullshit

There was a point in my life where I thought I knew it all. I was once told that the one who is no longer green, is dead. I wasn't sure what that meant but what I have chalked up is, if you're not willing to learn, you may as well hang up your hat and give up. There is also a saying that if you're the smartest one in the room, you're in the wrong room. I guess we have a lot to learn.

There is always something to learn and a lot of times especially for entrepreneurs and professionals, our egos tell us we have the answer even though we don't. I write these books from my experiences and I'm certain that I don't have all the answers. My

WINNERS WIN. LOSERS MAKE EXCUSES.

teachings are just based of what I have learned thus far. The crazy thing about this 'science' is that new variables I experience in life will change my perspectives, in turn changing my message.

As professionals we make decisions every day. I have taught people to make their decisions from intuition rather than from thinking through their decision, because especially in business, decisions need to happen quickly and the quicker you make these decisions, the quicker the outcome. You may make a mistake and fail, but what you learned gears you for quicker decision making down the line. Experience is key in business and in life. However, you must be open to learn new things and new perspectives.

Listen to your peers and customers. They will tell you what's up. If a client complains, they may be wrong, but listen anyway. See their side of the situation. There is something to learn there. If you turn a blind eye, your arrogance will get the best of you. If you continue to hear the same complaint over and over and you're not listening, the answer or solution is right in front of you and you're oblivious to it. If you truly feel that you have the best product or service, you're setting yourself up for a huge wake up call. Believe me, I have been there. The last thing you want is a flood of complaints destroying your reputation.

I was just looking at the website for Paul Hollywood from The Great British Baking Show and it says in big letters right on the home page, "The Best Baker in the Country". The idea of being the best in the country is just him stroking his own ego. I found it very tasteless and quite a turn off. Below that are his books for sale which I will not be buying. Now, let's flip

WINNERS WIN. LOSERS MAKE EXCUSES.

the script. Had it said, "World Renowned Baker with 30 Years Experience", and this his books below, at that point, I could take an interest because I know there is something to learn. I'm sure there is a lot to learn from the "Best Baker in the Country", but how much of that book is him tooting his own horn and what is the cause and effect of ego stroking at that level? Is the issue that he doesn't believe in himself? Is the issue that he wants to be the best so in order to be the best, he has say he's the best? Is it just a marketing ploy? We see this all the time.

Real estate professionals, dentists, car dealerships, authors, etc claim they are the best in the world or in this case, the best in the country. Technically, I could say I am the best cold caller in the world because I wrote the multi best-selling book The Cold Call King, but I know deep down there are much much better sales people out there. The question then lies, what makes somebody better than somebody else and where does ethics play a role in the scenario? I know cold callers that will always close the deal but they are bending the truth and selling shit to people that don't actually need what is being sold to them. So, does that make them better? Yes and no, right?

If you're a liar, you're a liar. If you're a fool, you're a fool. If you truly don't know and a mistake was made, you have something to learn and staying green will get you there. But believing the bullshit you spew and saying it's your way or the highway, you're setting yourself up for a really low point in your life. Whether now, in a year or on your deathbed, your time will come. Keep you eyes, ears and mind open and always be learning. You're either green or you're dead.

WINNERS WIN. LOSERS MAKE EXCUSES.

There is also the people that just want to hear themselves talk. They read something and spew the same garbage over and over to everybody they come across but don't know the cause or effect of the matter. We see this with MLM people or real estate 'investors'. Earlier today, I was speaking with one of my investors in my circle and he was telling me how many people he comes across that may have purchased their first home or may not have ever purchased real estate and they are calling themselves real estate investors, selling seminars and real estate training. Isn't there laws against this? Clearly, there isn't.

We see this in a variety of industries. Business coaches that take a class and get a certificate call me and want me to train them on how to build their business, yet they are charging people to help them build theirs. The sad part is, when I sit down with

WINNERS WIN. LOSERS MAKE EXCUSES.

these people, a lot of them don't know shit about building a business. What's even worse, a lot of them can't afford to pay my invoice. I have had people borrow money from parents to pay me the $600 for the two-hour session. Most times, I won't even take their money. Two hours isn't going to get them much and taking their last $600 just doesn't seem ethical to me.

When you encounter somebody that you think is feeding you a load of baked beans, remember to listen to their story they are telling you rather than the words. Chances are, their words will tell you one thing as the story will tell you something else. I always use the analogy Mary had a little lamb when I refer to this exercise. If you listen to the words of Mary had a little lamb, it will tell you she had a lamb. But, if you listen to the story of Mary had a little lamb, it will tell you she still has a lamb. The people you need in society will

WINNERS WIN. LOSERS MAKE EXCUSES.

tell you the same thing. They may say business is good, but if they are having issues paying an invoice, chances are, business isn't so great.

A New Start

If you have made it this far in this book, something has probably resinated with you piquing your interest. Whether you've been an entrepreneur for decades or are just starting out, part of staying green is identifying habits and places you can improve. When I write a book, I try not to sugarcoat anything. I admit, I don't have all the answers and I will admit when I am wrong, however I do try to bring as much fact to my writing rather than opinion, unless of course it's a political piece. I am constantly learning everyday. I speak to professionals daily and hear their stories and identify their patterns and areas for

WINNERS WIN. LOSERS MAKE EXCUSES.

improvement, and these along with my own lessons is my inspiration in writing a book like this.

When I wrote my first business book, it wasn't to stroke my ego or to see my name in lights. I had people coming to me with the same problems over and over and I honestly just didn't have time to sit with all of them. I had to systemise it somehow and print was the best way to do this. I wish I could've been able to sit down with each of them to tackle those issues because I love these types of interactions, but my phone was ringing from across the globe. Remember, I was the guy on the radio. There was an audience listening and they had a lot of questions. I knew that writing books discussing different business topics would be helpful, but I didn't know that we would be selling books to business schools and sales departments. It was quite flattering to be honest, but

WINNERS WIN. LOSERS MAKE EXCUSES.

ultimately I am just glad I can use my experiences and talents to help people.

Getting a new start doesn't have to be a new start per se, it can be identifying one area you want to improve. Maybe, you already knew the lesson written in this book, but over the years, you found comfort in taking risks. Those risks then turned into habits and those habits became the norm. Remember, we all do the same things. We're all looking for shortcuts in order to stay efficient and competitive. Don't think that anything you're doing is wrong, unless of course, you're ghosting clients and missing appointments. That's no good. But now, after reading this book, you've identified where maybe you have gone wrong and want to get back on track. We can all improve in many ways and each little improvements makes us THAT much better.

WINNERS WIN. LOSERS MAKE EXCUSES.

They say practice makes perfect. But, what happens when you practice wrong? Well, it just makes you really good at doing it wrong. Finding even one area from this book that could improve your life will take a little work to execute. Find one area, for instance, punctuality and not canceling appointments is a big one. By arriving early to your next ten or fifteen appointments will set the standard moving forward. If you cancel or reschedule even one of those appointments, it takes you back to your old ways with no improvement to your accountability.

When you wake up in the morning, take a deep breath and make your bed. Then, take a shower and enjoy the moment. If you have kids going crazy in the other room, level with them and explain to them that you need a minute to yourself. You're probably rolling your eyes in this moment saying to yourself, this isn't how it works. BUT, if you got up twenty minutes

WINNERS WIN. LOSERS MAKE EXCUSES.

before your kids did and took your shower, you now have your time to yourself and are calmer in the day, leading to a more productive day. You're less rushed in the morning. You got the kids off to school. You took the scenic route to work by the little lake with the ducks, and stopped for coffee. You did all of this with the extra twenty minutes from waking up a little earlier. Only your excuses will prevent this from happening.

After a long day at work, you're a little more relaxed. You come up, get the kids situated and tucked in, climbing into your freshly made bed to do it all again tomorrow. Yet tomorrow, you set your clock for another ten minutes early. We all have plenty of time in the day to do the things we need to do and enjoy life, we just choose to create excuses for our bad habits because we live in the moment and don't think about the consequences, regardless of how small they can be.

Being rushed leads to stress on the body. You don't eat before work, you drive as fast as you can to a job you hate, or love, risking an accident and you're stressed at work, coming home and taking it out on your kids. They misbehave because they aren't getting what they need from mom and dad which stresses you out further creating a cycle of disfunction. Kids react to your energy. If you're all wound up, your kids aren't going to sit there quietly. It just doesn't work like that. If you have an orderly house and have respect in the home, chances are your kids will be little shits when they aren't in your presence. They will feed off the energy of who they are around. And, if you're working all the time and don't know who they are around, well then you can't get upset when they are with people you don't want them to be around.

So, what does all this mean? Start with you. Start with creating new habits. Start by writing down what you want to accomplish with your work or business. This also affects your life too, so write down what you want in life as well. Then, write down where you think you need improvement. If you don't think you need improvement, start with why you don't think you need improvement and realise your ego needs a little work. Believe me, we all have an ego. Sometimes it gets the best of us.

Once you have identified where you can improve, start implementing little changes into your life. Waking up earlier, making your bed, enjoying you time, slowing down, treating yourself to coffee, listen to audiobooks on the way to the office instead of the morning show on the radio. Fill your brain with

WINNERS WIN. LOSERS MAKE EXCUSES.

positive content. Surround yourself with positive people. Cut out the garbage you're feeding yourself and see where it takes you.

Something I learned recently was, how often do you do things for you? When was the last time you took yourself on a date? Have you ever done that? Saying you don't have time is an excuse. There is always time for yourself if you allot it for yourself. Taking yourself to a cup of coffee or an ice cream or even just have lunch with the ducks feeding them part of your sandwich is so so good for your mind, body and soul. You'll release stress, you'll appreciate the natural beauties of the world and you'll find yourself less on edge with people which improves relationships.

It won't happen all at once. It will take a little here and a little there. Look at who you're friends with. Where are you spending your time? Do you go to the

WINNERS WIN. LOSERS MAKE EXCUSES.

bar on Friday night? Well, that's a great place to start. If you're pissing your money away on booze and surrounding yourself with a bunch of drunks, well then, I think you know what you expect of your life.

If you can take one thing from this book, remember this… Winner's win and losers make excuses. Winner's will always win because when they lose, they pivot and identify the lesson and strive for more. And losers will lose and find an excuse why they lost and will come to terms with the loss and give up. Which one are you?

Quit Making Excuses

Want to throw your life away? Then keep making excuses for yourself. Let's go over some of the best excuses I have heard recently.

Oh I could never do that. You're absolutely right. You could never do that IF you don't apply yourself. The problem here is the root of the statement. If you use fail words in your thinking, you will always fail. In this statement, the root is 'never'. By saying 'never', you immediately shut out the possibility of success or achievement. As an example, people tell me all the time they would love to write a book but could never do it. Why? Why can't you do it? Because you're lazy? Because you have a family to

WINNERS WIN. LOSERS MAKE EXCUSES.

feed? Because you have a busy job? A lot of my writing happens in the car. I am sitting in my car right now as I write this waiting to head into a client meeting. I found time to write. A lot of times, I will be in traffic with my notepad open on my phone and using dictation software speaking my thoughts into my phone and using that to write my books. Let's get into our next excuse.

I don't have time. You would be surprised to know what you actually have and don't have time for. Do you watch TV? Well, then you have time. Why do I keep pointing blame at television? Because it's a time suck. Because a half hour or hour of television takes up a lot more of your life than you think. **But TV relaxes me before bed**. So would writing down your thoughts and your accomplishments. Have you ever wondered why there aren't Lamborghini or Bentley commercials on television? The answer might shock you. The answer is also quite simple. The people who buy and own Lamborghinis and Bentleys don't watch much television. It's not that they don't have time to watch TV, they just focus their energy on things that bring value and quality to their life. Like I said before, if you prioritise your time and focus on things that bring you value, then you are able to give the world more of you, making you more valuable to others.

I can't afford it. Oh this one gets me every time. I learned this one from one of Robert Kiyosaki's books. What I love so much about books is, you learn from the wisdom of others without taking decades of your life making the same mistakes. This is why I write so many books. I know that when I am gone, my wisdom will still be here helping others for generations to come. So, our excuse... I can't afford it. For one, our root of the excuse is 'can't'. By implying you can't do something, you immediately throw the idea of possibility out the window. Instead, maybe ask "how can I afford it?" At that point, you create the idea of what it will take to accomplish the goal and if you still feel that it doesn't make sense, then you have a real reason as to why you don't want to move forward.

I have always wanted to buy a Bentley but the thing that keeps coming back to me is a) the maintenance and b) putting a target on my back every time I go somewhere. Can I afford the car? Technically, yes. Do I want to spend my money on the car? Not really. Maybe someday when I have money to throw away, sure. But right now, I am just going to drive my Mercedes. It gets the job done. I have given considerable thought to Bentley ownership and the factor that scares me the most is sitting in traffic and being carjacked or even worse, my wife being carjacked. Living in the big city, nice cars and people wearing nice jewellery and being robbed in traffic for my watch just doesn't sound like fun.

You're just lucky. This one I have heard many times in my life. Let me tell you, there is no luck in my life. There has never been a 'right place at the right time'. Every single thing I have, even my wife, was earned the hard way. Here's a funny story about my wife and I.

I met her on a dating site many many years ago, way before there were dating apps. I must have emailed her a dozen times before she responded. She says the only reason she responded was because she was bored and I truly believe that. She was 23 and enjoying life and I was 30 looking for a wife. Two completely different ideals in life at the time. The irony is, once we met, we never left each other's side. We have always been there for each other. I was living in my car after losing my motorcycle shops. She was living at home with her folks. Pretty much everything I've built today, her and I did together.

In my 25 years as an entrepreneur, I have built probably 50 businesses. From selling Ferrari parts and motorcycle helmets to shooting movies and producing music to writing books and even attempting to build a TV network, we did it together. I even worked with Google for a while building an entrepreneur-based search engine. I've done it all. There is been no luck.

There's a saying successful people will tell you. It took 20 years to be an overnight success. There are a few circumstances where people hit it big, but even then, there was trials and lessons to be learned. The guy that wins $100 million in the lottery, that isn't a blessing. That is a curse. This guy has no idea how to

WINNERS WIN. LOSERS MAKE EXCUSES.

manage that kind of money. Family will come out of the woodwork, IRS will have a fun time with them, he will want to cover his depression with spending sprees which will only fuel deeper depression. Nothing is free in life and there is no such thing as luck. There is only investment. You must invest and the more you invest in yourself, the more you will get in the long run.

I watched a video the other night about an old man in Ecuador who sold Coconuts on the street corner. I think they called him The Coconut Man. He said he has no money and no home but is happy because that's all he has. Without happiness, we have nothing. Was he lucky to be alive? We all deserve to enjoy our life, long or short. This charity group came up and gave him money and a home and a future. Was it luck? I don't think so. He earned that. Through the joy and love he gave others, his

WINNERS WIN. LOSERS MAKE EXCUSES.

sacrifices in life gave others the inspiration they needed to better their lives and in turn, the charity rewarded him. There was no luck there. Just the investment in himself rewarded by the investment of others.

It's too hard. Nothing in life is easy. Tell me one thing in life that is easy. Writing books? Though it has come pretty natural to me, I have had to take the time to master my craft and invest in myself. I was never good in school. I didn't come from a family of scholars. I was an abused kid with parents which neither went to college.

I enjoy writing books. I enjoy story telling. I enjoy inspiring and motivating people through my experiences. You're probably reading this and wondering why my grammar sucks and why I don't use proper comma placement, that's because I'm uneducated. It's not an excuse. My work is an extension of me. I can use editors but choose not to. There's a ton of software programs out there that could polish my writing, but I feel it would lose the edge and rawness of my writing. However, I am wise. I have learned everything I know from reading and trial and error and my gift to the world is the wisdom I can bring others.

The idea of giving up because something is hard only hurts where life will take you. With my ventures over the years, they have all been hard. There are trials. There are times I don't know what moves to make. There are times, I'm not sure where life is taking me. I just stay the course and focus on what I want to achieve. I continue to set new goals for myself and let life happen. We really have little control over where life takes us, but God has a plan. The universe has a plan. Something has something in store for us. We just need to follow our intuition and use our talents and skills to see where life is taking us. But making excuses and leaning on laziness is the last thing you want to do IF you want to be successful.

And sitting here waiting for my 11a to show up, she's late. I'm sure she has a great excuse. Winners will win. Losers will make excuses.